A Quarter Dead
and Half Alive

STEVE DENEHAN

RENARD PRESS

RENARD PRESS LTD

124 City Road
London EC1V 2NX
United Kingdom
info@renardpress.com
020 8050 2928

www.renardpress.com

A Quarter Dead and Half Alive first published by Renard Press Ltd in 2025
For individual dates of first publication see Acknowledgements on p. 205.

Text and cover illustration © Steve Denehan, 2025

Printed and bound in the UK on carbon-balanced papers by CMP Books

ISBN: 978-1-80447-160-9

9 8 7 6 5 4 3 2 1

CLIMATE POSITIVE Renard Press is proud to be a climate positive publisher, removing more carbon from the air than we emit and planting a small forest. For more information see renardpress.com/eco.

EU Authorised Representative: Easy Access System Europe – Mustamäe tee 50, 10621 Tallinn, Estonia, gpsr.requests@easproject.com.

Contents

A QUARTER DEAD

AND HALF ALIVE

For my family and friends,
and for Will, for taking a chance.

Flickering

I see the candle flame
flickering
from one hundred yards away

yet I know
that if I were to hold the candle
it would illuminate
almost nothing

The Pebble

The beach was deserted
had been left to us
by even the seagulls

the sand was still warm in the evening sun
we grabbed at it with our toes
as we stood
at the water's edge

there were no sounds
the horizon was empty and wide
wide enough that we could see
the curve of the Earth

somewhere beyond it
there were all sorts of things
bad, good
the life that we had left behind
temporarily at least

I felt my daughter at my side
her upturned face was smiling
she held a pebble in her hand
told me that it was the smoothest pebble in the world
I took it from her
moved it between my thumb and forefinger
she was right

The Bird Feeder

I don't know much about birds
but I watch them flit
to and from the bird feeder

they are small and mostly brown
there are some with yellow throats
there are robins
there are others
that might be starlings

they move in jitters
their heads turning left and right
right and left
stop-motion animation
in our back garden

it is winter but spring is at its edges
the air is still
the sky is blue
the sun shines

the birds flit
to and from the bird feeder
I notice that there are pheasants
two of them
standing underneath
waiting for the seeds to fall

Bright Blue

There is a crowd
small but growing
looking out to sea

despite the storm
I walk over
collar up, head down

people point
some are shouting
others look away

I follow the fingers
see nothing but the waves
wild and heaving

a man, talking on the phone
runs his fingers
through his hair

I look again
out to sea
nothing, nothing

something
a piece of wood
a strip of metal, maybe

a body
a body
a body

lifeless, far below
far away
unreachable

squinting, I see
long hair, a bright blue dress
the white of her face

the water rises
she rises with it
and we

can only watch
and point
and look away

Fishing Line

He can't remember yesterday
or the yesterdays before
but he can remember a Wednesday afternoon
in 1949
he can remember pain
burning cold
unrelenting

the pores in the face of his father
inches from his own
tobacco on his warm, soft breath
tying fishing line around the tooth
his mother singing along to the radio in the other room
the stain on the wallpaper
near the ceiling
the shape of Africa

his father patting him on the shoulder
walking to the open door
tying the fishing line to the handle
the room swaying with nerves and courage
'Ready?'
nodding
each of them taking a breath
the world stopping

he remembers
the door
slamming

how the fishing line had been invisible
until that moment
before it sprung taut and caught the sun
he remembers the tooth landing on the carpet
pure white on dull brown
he remembers one pain replacing another
the taste of an old penny
his father bending to retrieve the tooth
offering it to him on his calloused palm
asking if the pain had gone
he remembers nodding a lie

The Chevrolet

The rain has been falling all morning
straight down
sky to earth
sheets of it, so heavy
as to not be swayed by the wind

I am getting a new car tomorrow
trading in my Chevrolet
for a Renault
American for French
petrol for electric
old for new

the Chevrolet saw me through eleven years
has a mess of miles on the clock
is as aerodynamic as a brick
but it started every time and never failed
to take me to
and away

J.D. Salinger said of poets
that they always take the weather personally
that they stick their emotions
into things that have no emotion

he is right
still, I hope it will be sunny tomorrow

Sharing a Sink with
John. B. Keane in a Pub Toilet
in the Mid-Nineties

I am rarely in a pub
I had never been in Kerry
but that evening I found myself
in a pub in Tralee

sent scurrying
by the smallest of talk
to a cubicle in the pub toilet
to sit there
killing time

people came and went
while I read graffiti
in a stench
thick as soup

eventually, I steeled myself
opened the cubicle door
walked to the sink to wash my hands
when in *he* walked

John B. Keane
eyes hooded, nose long, shoulders sloped
older, but the same
he stood beside me at the sink

winked at me in the mirror
reached into his suit jacket
pulled out a toothbrush
and a tube of toothpaste

started to talk in his heavy accent
a dozen words a second
brushing his teeth, all the while
toothpaste foaming on his lips

I told him that I had read *Sive*
and, with his eyebrows high
he spat into the sink
and asked if I had liked it

I paused
too long
much too long
his laughter shook the cubicles
the palm of his hand landed hard on my back, and
as I watched the toilet door
slowly close behind him
he was laughing still

Room to Room to
Room to Room

Bone tired
after a thirteen-hour sleep
I wander the house
in a semi stupor

lurching, hollow legged
room to room
to room to room
I don't know

what is wrong with me
when it came
when it will pass
what I do know is that

everything is changing
has changed and
I am a ghost
haunting only myself

Pickpecking

While the water boils
I look out the kitchen window
there is no breeze, and so
little movement

still, as I settle into a trance
I notice small birds flitting
from branch to feeder
pickpecking seed

the kettle clicks
the water, which has been bubbling
stops

in the silence I pour the boiled water
into a mug
that contains a teabag

I stir the teabag until the tea is released
until the water is brown

I remove the teabag and pour
a little milk until the brown
becomes lighter

when I was younger
I would take two teaspoons of sugar
maybe three
now, I take none

I read somewhere once
that there is a certain freedom to be found
in giving up
I have not found this to be true

In the Cutlery Drawer

She tells me that she loves my poems
which brings the hated question
'Why don't you write some too?'
her face is calm, but I feel the change
'I can't, I don't know how.'
and so, our dance begins
sometimes a gentle sway
more often, a blazing tango
'I can't! I don't know how!'

she leaves me notes to find
on scraps of cereal boxes
under the kettle
      'I can't wait to be home.'
in the cutlery drawer
      'I miss you.'

poetry, the purest kind
diamonds to my glass

Mount Carmel Maternity Ward,
January 2012

3 a.m., 4 a.m.
holy hours
hours when we sat together
the three of us
a new family
in the bowels
of the hospital
we looked down at her
her eyes shut tight
her mouth opening and closing
lips softly smacking
looking for the nipple
finding it
but not latching on
the worry then
that she might never discover
how to latch on
how to bring the life into her
knowing now
that she did
and never stopped

Saltwater Rising

I step into the ocean
ice water elongating my feet
I walk forward
freezing saltwater rising
finding, invading
every part of me

I keep on walking
until I stand
on the tips
of my toes
winter water swelling
underneath my chin

I stay there for a while
half held
until I am not so cold

2013, Before Dementia

A nothing year
unremembered
by everyone

a drop
in a puddle of other
unremembered years

the year my father
was seventy-six
the year that I

was thirty-eight
half his age, and he
twice mine

a one-time thing
a small thing
in a nothing year

I have gained on him
in the years since, while he
has moved further and further away

Lunchtime in Dublin City

A stiff, cold breeze
the promise of snow behind it
I walk fast to keep warm
turn up the music in my earphones
to drown out the traffic
and the people
and my thoughts
and it works
almost

an hour to kill and nowhere to go
I see a guy from work
a real sickener from the third floor
walking towards me
talking to him on company time is hard enough
I duck into the nearest shop
grab a pastry, join the queue
the cashier looks tired
she is fifteen years older than me, or so
goes through the motions until
it is my turn
I hand her my pastry
the barcode doesn't work, and the manager takes it away
the cashier smiles, makes small talk
it takes a while, and the queue grows
the cashier becomes nervous
I don't know why
she asks if I would like to go out sometime
I hold up my hand, show her my ring

tell her that I'm sorry
she shakes her head, it's OK
says that she gets lonely
that I seem nice

the manager returns, the barcode works
I say goodbye and walk away
the sickener is in the queue a few back
he chuckles
for no reason that I can see
tells me to wait for him outside
I don't want to
but I do
I stand there on Grafton Street
blowing hot air into my cold hands
the whole of the sky is white
I want to cut the skin of it
want all the snow to fall at once
filling up the streets until everything is gone

How to Raise a Daughter

I would burp
she would laugh
we would look at each other
smiling

I would burp again
she would laugh again
it never got old
until it did

now, when I burp
she rolls her eyes
so *I*
blame *her*
and she laughs

but I know
that this won't last
and honestly
I don't know where to go from here

The Tin

Sometimes I come upon it, the tin
small but weighty, slightly mysterious

once, long before me, it was a biscuit tin
now, the lid is chipped and worn
the colours tired
years might pass before it is seen
forgotten, then remembered

I was a boy that first time
slowly, silently pulling the lid off
hoping for secret treats
finding instead a dense, shimmering treasure
buttons
so many buttons

she told me that she had started collecting them before
before me
before my father
before almost everything and everyone
before

silver, gold and brass
some tarnished, some gleaming
some small and subtle
from the times she was unsure
still finding herself
some large and ornate
that could only be worn by a woman

who has learned to lean into the wind
instead of being blown away

this time I find it in the hot-press
in dusty dark recesses
it harboured part of my childhood
and all of hers
my fingers find it
before my eyes, and I
am tumbling through lifetimes

slowly, silently, I pull off the lid
there they were
there they are
buttons
so many buttons
one is blue
the blue of her still twinkling eyes
'Each one is a memory,' she says, startling me

the box is nearly full

Traffic

We are a multicoloured metal glacier inching towards the sun. I
can't understand why the guy behind me is so close. We are going
nowhere. Doesn't he get that? I look to my left. An older lady, too
old for this, clings to her steering wheel and stares straight ahead.
I look to my right and see a guy, about my age, but in better shape,
talking animatedly. To an empty car. Handsfree. I hope. I turn up the
music, hoping it will enter me through my pores. Hoping it will wash
me away. But I am made of stone today and I realise my teeth are
clenched together as we inch and inch and inch. Stop. Start. Stop.
Start. There is a slight   quickening   but   I   remind   myself
not   to   get   too   excited,   that   it   might   mean   nothing,
another   false   alarm.   I   can   sense   it   though,   among
us,   adrenaline   in   the   air,   like   pollen,   and   we
breathe   it   in   and   I   feel   my   right   foot   tingle,
ready   to   finally   hit   the   floor.   We   gather   pace,
slowly   at   first   but   I   think   this   is   it,   it
is   happening   and   we   are   moving   and
the   cars   begin   to   pull   away   from
each   other   as   we   awaken   together
and   our   hearts   are   loud
but   our   engines   louder   as
we   roar,   screaming,
into   the   sun.

The Whistling Man

Nobody knows what I did
just five minutes ago and now
I walk down the street
and nobody knows

ahead of me a well-dressed couple walk
he, talking too much
she, aloof and disinterested
I know how that ends

a homeless man sleeps in the doorway of a derelict building
I wonder if the homeless dream
perhaps he is not asleep at all

cars pass by driving to and driving from
a policeman stops me
'Sir, you have some blood on your shirt…'
I reassure him, 'A nosebleed, I am fine.'
he smiles, I smile
and on and on I walk

I am invincible – almost invisible – just this morning I
was God, and still, I feel that fury move
up and move down me

while I wait for the elderly lady to give me my change
a cat snakes around and through my legs
'He likes you.'

'He has very poor taste!'
she laughs, I laugh, we laugh
she has no idea

I keep walking, I do not think I will ever get tired
it is as if I am breathing in raw ozone
I think I can smell the electricity coming from within me
I hear someone whistling and it takes me a moment to realise
that it is me, and people smile

they are not afraid, not of the whistling man
they do not know
nobody knows
like Jesus, and Lucifer, I walk among them
nobody knows what I have done
as bluebirds turn and fly into the sun

A Match in Mount Merrion, Dublin, Twenty-Seven Years Ago

I remember the rain
angry
unyielding
wild and loud and pointed
the referee talking about calling it off
we stood on the pitch
we stood *in* the pitch
ankle deep
jerseys clinging to us
hands on our hips
shaking our heads
wet to our bones
as the referee blew his whistle

it was a war
blood for mud
bellows and whistles
every yard
hard won
the pitch was carved and gouged
knees and elbows
sliding tackles
everything given
for a nothing match
I think we won
or lost
or drew

A Poem from My Father
to My Mother

Remember when we met
when I was a kite
when you were the wind
when Dublin was dance-hall days
foggy nights
what-ifs and maybes

remember when I fell into myself
how you forgave me
and forgive me still
remember Burt Bacharach in the hotel lobby
when you exclaimed, 'It's *him!*'
remember how we used to dance
how the room spun with us
This Guy's in Love with You
remember when you said, 'Yes.'

remember those funhouse mirror years
when you remained a childless mother
remember the worry in your voice
when you threw the word into the air
not knowing if I would catch it
'Adoption…'
remember how I was the fool
who should have held you
more

remember how they grew
in our arms
on our laps
how they left
but never leave
remember when months became decades
and we forgave ourselves
for getting old

remember before

I started

to forget

remember when we ran across the dawn
or wanted to, at least

A Dark Spot, Glistening

I went walking today
not something I do
usually

especially not under a low sun
in crackling windless air
still, I went walking

it didn't take long
to feel the trickle of sweat
rolling down
between my shoulder blades

even less time
for my fingers
to come away slick
from my forehead

behind me in the distance
was a cyclist
gaining slowly
without looking I knew
that it was him
the farmer

he stopped beside me
I could see that underneath his jacket
was another jacket
a jumper and a shirt

we talked a while
well, he talked
I listened
or rather
nodded

a few minutes went by
before he climbed on to his bicycle
told me that he had enjoyed the chat
and I watched him cycle away
as the world trembled in the heat

my mouth was dry
but I spat on the ground even so
watching it land on the yellow dirt
a dark spot, glistening
in just a minute or two
it would disappear

Sitting on a Bench, Waiting

I didn't know him, not really
a nod hello, the weather
he worked on the floor above
might have been five years older
it was hard to tell
what with all the weight
that he had on him
what with his face
free of wrinkles
the skin stretched taut
over jowls and chins

an enormous man
so heavy that to estimate his weight
required a five-stone swing
twenty to twenty-five, or so
he smiled a lot
all teeth, a little too eager
kept himself to himself

he went away one summer
two weeks, to Thailand, alone
came back married
the lads laughed about it over lunch
I saw the wedding photo on his desk
displayed proudly
she was a foot shorter
two feet narrower

years went by; another photograph appeared
a daughter, beautiful
later, another, a smiling boy
I thought about his wife
thought that this
was way above
and way beyond

I sat in the park one spring lunchtime
reading my book and eating a sandwich
he sat on a bench, waiting
I saw the light in him as they approached
his children played on the grass
saw him clap his hands at their awful cartwheels
his wife looked at him
slipped her hand into his
I got back to my book and left them to it

A Worm in 1981

I am a worm
having burrowed under the covers
deep
to the bottom of my bed
I lie there, curled
the mattress pressing up into me
the blankets pressing down upon me
breathing
until the air is gone
until the only air left
is my own
and I take it
hot and damp
back into myself
in quick, shallow gulps

looking around
in that quiet dark
I hear the door open
feel my father's hand
through the blankets
on the small of my back
and I understand
even then
that it is impossible
to disappear completely

His Name Escapes Me
Right Now but It Might Come Back
to Me Later

They gave him everything
water torture
sleep deprivation
they starved him
removed his fingernails
the fingers themselves
his ears
they peeled parts of his forearms and thighs
dripped acid on to his feet
cut words across his chest and stomach

his motorcade had driven
too close to enemy lines
he had been captured
a bounty, a piñata
bulging
with military secrets

held for months
presumed dead
forgotten by most
until his body
what was left of his body
was returned

it is believed
that he gave them nothing
that he endured it all
everything they had
and gave them nothing
maybe nothing was all he had to give
maybe it was that simple
either way his family
their knees worn smooth from prayer
got him back

at his funeral there were flags, and
a twenty-one-gun salute
that frightened his son
his family were given a medal
to honour his bravery
it was shiny

Midnight at the Petrol Pump

Pump in hand
trigger pulled
I breathe it in
the fumes
the forecourt
an illuminated box
of cold light
the faces, few, tired
Muzak plays
sounding far away
I see him then
an old colleague
from an old job
he looks much the same
a little greyer
a little rounder
the usual
I wait for him to turn
for us to catch eyes
he doesn't
we don't
I see my face reflected in the car window
a little greyer
a little rounder
the usual
the slam of his car door
takes me from my trance
and I watch him drive away
into all that dark

April Sun

The weather is to hold
the farmer tells me

we face each other
a row of gorse between us

he does not move
the way he used to

a stiffness has set in
bringing slowness with it

we talk
how we always talk

about the past
his past

before he picks up
the sack of meal, and looks

to the far end
of the field

where cattle wait
expectantly

the weather is to hold
he says again

Naming Snowflakes

I told her that she would run out
but she was adamant and so
we lay on the ground
looking straight up
as the snow fell as embers
through the streetlight

she pointed at a snowflake
'Mary!'
at another
'John!'
at another
'Jane!'

a snowflake later
maybe two
the names dried up
I laughed
she became angry
I laughed harder
she nudged me
with her elbow

we lay there for a while
watching
in the snowy quiet

'I wish the snow could fall for ever, Dad.'

barely a whisper

I think the last flake
was called Jemima

Procrastinator

Yesterday I put off dinner
until the day slipped by and so
I went without

today I got up and told myself
that I would do my run early
get it out of the way
freeing myself up
for the rest of the day

instead, I found other things to do
emptying the tumble-dryer lint tray
reorganising the bathroom cabinet
watching YouTube nonsense
leaving my run as late as possible
at which point
the world was grey, and it was raining

instead of jumping into the shower after
I sat in the kitchen, saturated
playing a pool video game
on my phone
until I was stiff and the cold
was through me

the dishes are piled high in the sink
the clothes are stacking up
I tell my wife to leave them

that they are on my radar
that I will get to them
and I mean it
at the time

I had intended to write this poem
last week

The Great Writer
and His Process

A writer, a great writer
was asked for his secret
just how does he write
such powerful poems

he talked about his process
how he would find a quiet time
in a quiet room and fall
into a kind of meditation

during which he would search
deep within himself
earnestly trying to reach depths
previously unplumbed

he stated that often he would surprise himself
discover more about himself
free himself
from himself

it all sounded quite pretentious
but, stuck for a poem today and with nothing
to lose
I decided to try it

closing the sitting-room door behind me
I turned off my music
sat on the couch
opened the laptop

the silence was pure
pure enough that I could hear it
I closed my eyes and waited to tumble
into myself

minutes passed and it occurred to me
that the writer
great as he was
never explained what to do

when a person journeys
deep into themselves
to find
that there is nothing

Fists

It took me forty thousand punches to realise
forty thousand too many
sure, I landed a few, enough to take me to this ring
but he is quick as light and made of iron and his punches
his punches come, again, and again, and again

the fists of my father, my mother, my schoolmates, of God himself
the glancing blows, the blows of the children I saw for an hour
last Christmas eve

I am winded from two body shots unseen
I disguise it
but he knows – I look in his eyes – he knows
he comes for me, and though the ring is an infinite thing
I can find no place to hide

then, an opening, a tunnel for my right hand and
I watch my fist blur towards him and
feel the contact rock the columns of his temple and
he is dazed and he is mine and his eyes look through me
and I call upon that old right hand one last time
the hand that signed my title deeds, my wedding certificate
my divorce papers
the hand that held my babies
that held your face for that first kiss
my sledgehammer, my bomb, but
it is so heavy now
and the fuse won't light, and then, I know

two seconds pass
two seconds that will stretch over all my days
two seconds when it was all there, another world
two seconds when I betray myself, as I always do

and so I wait, with nothing left
to get what I deserve, and when he comes
I do not run, and I am baptised in a flood of fists

I fall through the roar of the crowd and am caught
by the blanket of childhood
the lights above are so bright, and so pure, and
just beyond my reach

I lie on my back and watch dozens of moths
in frenzied compulsion
fly head first into the lights again
and again, and again

Cables and Cement

I remember the fear
blooming to my edges
to the tips of the hairs on my arms

he rarely raised his voice
but the roars came
so loud that when they stopped
the absence of them left me shaking

seventy years ago, now
he had called for us
my brother and I
we ambled into the back garden to find him
collar open, sleeves rolled up
smile wide, eyes squinting in the long sun rays

'Time for another lesson, boys.'
he had taught us how to sharpen a chisel
how to melt lead to make toy soldiers
how to catch a jackdaw
that day was the day we learned to mix
and to lay
cement

we looked at each other
the three of us
smiled
got to it
didn't talk much

but he had a hell of a whistle
and I admired his forearms
tight bunches of cables rippling under tan skin

a small section of the path had emerged
cracked and broken
unwanted magic
from the late winter snow
when we had finished it was new again
perfectly smooth
a job well done
we looked at each other
the three of us
smiled
my hands were caked with concrete
I noticed a cut on my wrist
the blood was stark against the grey
I hadn't even felt it

our cat appeared
we watched in silence
nobody moved
nobody spoke
as it nonchalantly padded across the cement
eight slow-motion pawprints
my brother and I turned to our father

seventy years later, I can still see him
his face and eyes a furious red
the veins in his temple
pulsing angry worms
his neck, hard and thick and ready
for roars that came and kept on coming

then there was silence
he threw up his hands and eyes and arms
I heard him mutter
'I give up.'
and watched him walk away
into the house
into the sitting room
on to his armchair
where he burned
defeated
for the rest of the day

today my brother and I met at the old place
the first time in a while
we stood shoulder to shoulder
looked down
laughed to ourselves
as rainwater filled the pawprints
an empty, concrete day
he is gone, long gone
with us soon to follow

The Arcadia

It is not the wheelchair
but the blanket
across his lap
that tells me
he is old
he is very old

I push him along the seafront
the seafront of my childhood
his fatherhood, and
I discover
his youth

he tells me of the long journey
the long road
travelled with his friends
sixty years before

he tells me of the nights
the lights
the ballroom heaving

we walk on
until he stops a young man
to ask for directions
to The Arcadia

the young man looks at me
I look at him
before he tells us both
that he does not know it

later, online, I find it
a sprawling, majestic ballroom
twinkling in photographs
that are black and white

it had flourished
in the forties and fifties
before being destroyed by fire
in the early sixties

I see crowds five thousand strong
my father among them, possibly

I call him and tell him
that next time
we will find it

Just an All-Round
Good Guy

There are two people
inside me

it has always
been this way

one is kind, considerate
thoughtful and patient
he puts others first
stands up
for those
who cannot stand up
for themselves

he is comfortable
easy on himself
incapable
of holding grudges
infinitely capable
of forgiveness

he enjoys people
is comfortable
in every situation
he is unfailingly optimistic
flexible

responsible
invincible

just an all-round good guy

the other one
is me

A Good End
to a Good Day

She sits small
in the crook of my arm
her little hand
sometimes resting
on my thigh

we see out the day
watching a film
on the television

not far from the end
someone
gives the middle finger
to someone else

my daughter looks up
I look down
expecting the question

she asks what it means
not having seen it
before

I tell her
that one person
does it to another person
when they are cross

she nods

when the film ends
I ask her to clean her teeth
to go
to bed

she uncurls herself
from me
gets up from the couch
walks to the door
turns, and
with dusky porchlight
all around her
gives me
the middle finger

days, and whole lives
can hinge
on such things

Watching an Independent Film
with My Wife

Sometimes they are black and white
sometimes subtitled
always independent
always acclaimed

we watch them occasionally
my wife and I
to test ourselves
to see what we are missing

it's always the same
the film is boring
pretentious and slow and interrupted
by my wife

twenty minutes in − 'Nothing is happening.'
half an hour in − 'There is still nothing happening.'
forty-five minutes in − 'There's not enough dialogue.'
forty-six minutes in − 'There's too much dialogue.'
an hour in − 'I don't care how good the cinematography is.'
seventy minutes in − 'Everyone looks the same.'
eighty minutes in − 'Is that a new character?'
ninety minutes in − 'Most films would be over by now.'
two hours in − 'I know it's nearly over, but,
I don't mind giving up on it now if you don't.'

we watched one recently
it was OK, barely
which made it better than most

the ending was frustrating
it was unclear as to whether the central character
had lived or died
just before the credits rolled my wife said
'The credits better not roll now.'

I don't understand why it is arty
to leave a film so open-ended
it's not that I need everything wrapped up
clean and neat
but surely it's a cheap shot, cynical
a dirty trick
to have the viewer invest over two hours
only to leave them hanging

it reminds me of the time
when I jumped off a bridge in Portugal, and
just before I hit the water I

When the Soil Is Flooded
Worms Come to the Surface to Breathe

I sat on a park bench
a hard day's work behind me
a pond full of ducks before me
in threes and fours they glided on the water
though I knew that beneath
they were paddling furiously

to my right there was a lady and her son
he was young
over five
under ten
it was hard to tell

there was something unusual about him
something inconsistent in his movements
he spoke loudly
with his mouth and with his hands
he repeated words and sentences often
though they made just as much sense
the last time as the first time

his mother had to calm him
every few minutes she took his head
into her hands
pressed her forehead against his
whispered to him
I noticed that she never
brushed the breadcrumbs from her lap

it had rained all morning
and all afternoon
there were puddles on the paths
drops fell into them
from the overhanging trees
dozens of worms had come to the surface
the boy saw them
became excited
started to stamp on them
it was the only sound
his mother looked away

That That

Today my mother told me
that
as a child
I did not like
to be told
what to do

on the drive home
I realised
that that
has always been
the difference
between us

Sandalwood

Some foundation, concealer
a little rouge
a subtle lipstick
her reflection disappoints
lines, hard earned, unwanted
her reflection smiles
it helps

she dusts and tidies
arranges
rearranges
old photographs
of ghosts

she lights a candle
sandalwood
she vacuums
and sweeps
she polishes
and primps
her home
herself
just in case

Sarah Goodwelles

A friend request popped up
Sarah Goodwelles, a chef from Paris
living in Texas
supposedly
she didn't look like the others
wasn't posing coquettishly
seductively
as-good-as-naked-ly

Sarah Goodwelles was pleasant-faced
wore a dark grey, slightly formal raincoat
and stood awkwardly before a field of tulips
blue as her young eyes
she sent me a message
in sweetly broken English

'Hi, how are you?'
        'Do we know each other?'
'Not soon, but I note you are a writer. I like to reading.'
        'Me too.'
'I am from France but live to Texas two years.'
        'Some day I hope to visit Texas.'
'Do you like sex?'

she didn't look like the others
but she was
probably a middle-aged man
like me
sitting somewhere far away

with other middle-aged men or women
trying to get people on the hook
I didn't mind
money is tight all over

      'Who are you? Who are you really?'
'Does it matter?'
        'Maybe not.'

I closed the laptop and went to bed

Dawn

Look at Allenwood
soft and misty veiled
our windowsill cat
a shock of orange
the horizon
a cracked egg
yolk leaking

look at our little girl
the world beating in her
rubbing the night from her eyes
humming herself awake
look at me
undone
almost
by it all

As If the Stars
Were Not Enough

'It hurts to laugh', you said
and I stared into your eyes
until you grabbed at your side
with a pleading smile

your appendix had growled
just after Christmas
so, it, the only poison in you
was cut out

I sat by you in the oppressive warmth
watched you glow in that unnatural hospital light
'Happy New Year.'
'Our first.'
'Yes.'

I stepped out into the night
the last night, before the next
and walked towards Dublin City
still charming from a distance

stopping on O'Connell Bridge with the rest
I gazed upwards
the sky thundered and pulsed with neon
as if the stars were not enough

from an open car window
I heard James Taylor sing 'you can close your eyes'
but I knew that I couldn't
not then
even if I'd wanted to

I sit now, twenty years later, sipping sweet tea
alone in a dingy coffee shop
my book dog-eared
the cold sun made warm by the window

my eyes rest on the page but my mind is raindrops
landing on small memories
and I am outside myself, looking
stunned at the luck I have had

I watch the plume of icing sugar that escapes the
            pack as you close it
that hangs in the air
framed in a summer window
a sweet smoke signal of all good things

I am there when you wake in your hospital bed
after our daughter had been cut out of you
the birth having been complicated
before you both were taken away

'How is she?'
'I haven't seen her yet.'
'Why not?'
'I thought we should see her together.'
'You waited?'
'We should see her together.'

then, the sky is low, and the sun is high
and we are wending our way through Albufeira
I look at her skin, newly sallow
there is a bull ring in the distance

'Why do they kill the bulls, Dad?'
'Because they can.'
'That's not a good answer.'
'No, it isn't.'

later, I pass my fingers through the flame of a candle
it flickers, and through it
in the bending air
are the whites of her eyes

School Visit,
24th October 2019

I stood at the top of the class
thirty pairs of eyes on me
I clutched some notes on poetry
although what did I know, really
a hand was raised in question
'What makes a poem really good?'
seven-year-olds
what a question
I had no idea
I put it back to him
asked him what he thought
'Honesty.'
quick as a flash
Jesus

'We learned from each other.'
is what I could tell people later
half a truth, half a lie

a rusty autumn wind waited for me
but first, the teacher said
'Just one last question.'
a hand shot up like a rocket
stretching, reaching
a firework of fingertips
her question, not a question

'I love you.'
my daughter
not embarrassed, not at all
not yet

What Waits
around the Corner

It is easy to become jaded
worn out by routine
by the same old same old
as the years pass

my daughter is not quite ten
nowhere near jaded, and eager
for the new, for surprise

she bounds up to me
open-faced and wide-eyed
asks me to tell her something amazing
something that will blow her head off

for the first time, I find myself
drawing a blank
she waits expectantly
I pretend to think
as though pondering which
of the dozens, hundreds of magical facts
I might tell her

a small thing arrives eventually
carrying with it a parcel of sadness
as I consider that this
may be the last time
that I blow her mind

'Light travels in straight lines.
Sound travels in waves, like water.
That is why we can hear
what is happening behind us
but cannot see it.'

she is quiet, thoughtful
then excited
'Ah ha! So that is why we cannot see
around corners!

she skips into the rest of her day
leaving me glad in the understanding
that jaded as I sometimes am
I really do have no idea
what waits
around the corner

Remembering

The phone rings
it is my father
I enjoy our chats
though these days
he often mentions
that he has not seen me
for a long time
even though
we might have visited
the day before

these days
he often mentions
that he has no recollection
of the previous day
or week
that he cannot remember
what month it is or whether
it is morning
or evening

these days
feel longer
than they should
and I hate myself for wishing
that, even for a while
I could forget about it all

Diving

I borrow a breath and dive
off a rock, old as time
into lives I might have led

I taste the salt of goodbyes
of faded postmarks
of the fact that you don't care to notice now
the specks of dirt on your crockery

I close my eyes
feel the brush of carnival streamers
against my upturned face
muffled drums beat through me

the screech of tyres
the sudden stop
I am airborne, for ever
then
I feel the grit, clawing, burning
into my chest

I am a ghost, resting on the ceiling
I watch myself below
withered and wheezing
sagging under a thin white blanket

I am burning from the inside out
and return, gasping
like I always do

Photograph

I look at the photograph
curled at the corners
dulled by time
I look at her
my mother
old to me then
young to me now
I blink
look again
she is younger still

My Birthday

Several people have asked me
my wife, my parents, a friend
even my daughter
whether I feel older today
than yesterday
they think that I am joking
when I tell them
that I do

Thousands of Hours,
Millions of Minutes

I haven't played now
for a couple of years
but in the years before that
I played
a lot
a hell of a lot
two matches a week
on average
for thirty-five years
three and a half thousand matches
maybe more
at all sorts of levels
in all sorts of weather

the training sessions
the drills
hundreds of thousands of hours
maybe millions of minutes
with a ball at my feet
all of it
for absolutely nothing
yet
sometimes
in the dark
my head on the pillow
it is the last thing I think of

Soft Drizzle

She died yesterday
is still dead today
easy to accept
impossible to understand
she is dead
dead as can be
mortal
after all

there was a soft drizzle this morning
I breathed it in
felt it on the fur of our cat
as he pushed against my bare calf
purring as the cat food slid out of its pouch
landing in his bowl
with a wet plop
it is always the day after something

Morocco

The little boy reached down
picked up a white stone
held it towards me
'Five.'
I shook my head
having no change
'Two.'
I shook my head again
patted my pockets
held my palms to him

he understood
dropped the stone to the ground
walked away

later, walking back to the hotel
I saw him again
standing at the market entrance
we caught eyes
he nodded
I waved
he patted his pockets
held his palms towards me
I smiled
he smiled

I wonder where he is now
I wonder
where am I

Gentle

Getting up
from the armchair
is a process
for him
now

he steels himself
leans forward
grasps each arm
with mottled hands
swollen and arthritic

takes a breath
pulls himself slowly
and with great effort
up and up until
he is standing crookedly

the effort required
almost sends him
tumbling back into his chair
but there is still
some fight left in him

he stands, dithering
withering before me
my father
swaying and mumbling
lost in his Aran cardigan

Dylan Thomas said
'Do not go gentle
into that good night'
but sometimes
there is no other way

Hatch Street Years

I would wander through the record shops
they must have known me
must have been sick of the sight of me
every day
earphones in
flicking through the same old music
trying to forget
until I had to go back

the gentle hill of Grafton Street
felt steep
as I walked back up it
crossed over the road
into Stephen's Green
to envy the ducks
on up to Hatch Street
the tall, grey building
waiting, always waiting

a place of forced smiles
stale air
a waste of bricks
carpets, glass, plumbing
wires, paint, tile
of whole lives

sometimes I would stand outside
unable to enter
the sign above me

the smooth sound of the revolving door
brushing a marble floor
worth my annual wage
at least
it took all that I had
to step forward
into the profound, churning drudgery

I remember standing in the lift
with another guy
we both looked straight ahead
'It's a living.'
he said
and I thought
'Is it?'

Ducks

The forecast gave rain
but we
cycle in the sun
the canal beside us

from just over
my left shoulder
my daughter squeals

panic gives way quickly
to joy
as I follow her finger

ducks
lots of ducks

we stop
climb off our bikes
sit on the bank, and
watch

there are ducks
lots of ducks
ducklings too

my daughter mentions
that they look so peaceful

sitting, gliding
on the water

I do not mention
that what I see
are ripples
lots of ripples

Pal

He was a friend
of a friend
his handshake was decent
but that
was about it

we did our best
talking
here and there
between shots
as the pool balls cracked
and the night
wore on

somewhere along the way
he mentioned
an obscure film
one that very few people
had seen

I
being one
of the very few

he talked of the director
such a visionary
all that

he had it wrong
the director, I mean

so, stupidly
I told him

he stood up
off the shot he was cueing

looked me in the eye
'Whatever you say, pal.'

some people
are very easy
to hate

Buzzing

It had been a few years
a good few years
but there he was
waving, smiling
from the deli counter

he asked
what I had been up to
laughed when I said
not much

I returned the question
before remembering why
it had been a few years
a good few years

he talked
about his promotion(s)
his family
the achievements
of his children

as he talked
I thought
about how excited
my daughter had been
to find the first bumblebee
of the season

how she had called me
from the garage
just to show

how plump he was
buzzing aimlessly
unaware, of her, of me

there was a call
the deli server
the sandwich ready

the last thing I heard
another question
'Where does the time go?'
supposed to be rhetorical
I think
but
I had a fair idea

The Carnival

We never quite made it
to the carnival

we drove from early morning
through the afternoon
into the evening
until the needle fell
into the red
to empty

then
we walked
sometimes hand in hand
until the evening fell to night
and dew came to the grass

we got close
close enough to see the lights
but we are old, and we
are tired, and so
we sit and watch the Ferris wheel
roll slowly out to sea

Herself

She likes distance
likes to keep herself
to herself

likes her job
Healthcare Cleaning Operative
mopper and sweeper

to the doctors and most
of the nurses
she is invisible

the patients talk to her
sometimes, and sometimes
they give her their books

she likes to read
to search for herself
in the pages

it has become hard, the job
she is stiff in the evenings
stiff in the mornings too

her breath has shortened
over time, and
last night

she coughed
to find red petals
on her handkerchief

there are people
she could call
people who would listen, would help

but she likes distance
likes to keep herself
to herself

so she steels herself, and dives
into the ocean
to shelter from the rain

Neon

We sat on the hillside
the city beneath us
the grass was not damp
but would be soon

you talked more than I did
which suited me fine
the usual stuff
nothings
and slightly smaller nothings

I knew something was coming
had felt a change in the air
before you paused and said
in not-quite-a-whisper
that your wife
no longer loved you

I gave it what I had
asked the right questions
offered evidence
tentative reassurance
while thinking
that it might be true

I told you to talk to your sister
to your mother
to your old friends

I told you to talk
to really talk
and really listen
to her

silence fell on us then
long seconds became long minutes

I looked at the faraway neon signs
in the shop windows
wanted to show you
how bright they were getting
in the seeping dark
but I figured
you would read something into it

North Strand Summer –
Seventy-Five Years Ago

Regrets pile up
over eighty-five years
is what I would have thought

but there is one
that stands above the rest
for my father

he stands in his back garden
summer scabs on his knees
a blue sky above him

nothing
is more dangerous
than an idle boy

the airgun feels heavy
in his right hand
not a little boy any more

he looks up, squints
to see the sky
blighted by imperfection

a small dark shape
straight line moving
he points, pulls the trigger

disappointed by the retort
not thunderous
but effective

the shape starts to fall
panicked spiralling
a pigeon, one wing working

one wing limp
my father watches
watches it fall in silence

watches it land
not far from him
with a wet thud

unaware that the pigeon
dead as soon as it hits the ground
will live with him for ever

Boy A and Boy B

It used to be that Boy A would offer to take you dancing
on dizzy Dublin nights
he would collect you in his father's car
wearing his father's suit
his hands clinging to the steering wheel
where they would not be seen to shake

Boy B, slightly shyer, would offer to take you to the cinema
the Savoy, still new and decadent
hushed voices and the swish of velvet
as the curtains parted and you stepped through
perhaps, if he was feeling brave, he would offer to link you home
while wondering if you could feel
the tremble of his arm

now Boy A takes you into darkness syrup thick and filled
with dead grasshoppers and dead birds and dead everything
and Boy B lets him

Seven Years Old

Today was the day that she said
    'Daddy, you won't know the age that I die at'
we looked at each other for a while
    'Daddy, don't you have anything to say?'

I held out my hand
she took it
I squeezed
she squeezed back
I smiled
she smiled

I didn't have anything to say

Breaths

The wind came like a flood
our home creaked
in pained resistance
and we, together on the couch
trembling, smiling
in the stretched atmosphere

'Let's go out, Dad!'
      'It might be too dangerous.'
'It won't!'
      'You might get blown away.'
'I won't! I am a big girl now.'

we stood in the warm winds
leaned into them
and felt unseen hands hold us
press our clothes against us

we looked up to see holes torn in the sky
layers of clouds moving in parallax
swirling greys and whites
and underneath it all…
'Let's play tag!'
and between the winds
we were running

I could hear her laughter
cut through the howling

I could feel her gaining
catching me already
I struggled up another gear
and pulled away
for now, at least

lying on the trampoline
squeaking springs
groaning trees
dancing leaves
holding hands
'Can we play again, Dad?'

for the first time
I say it
I am my father
I say it
in all this air
'Just let me get my breath back.'

Most Likely

I did not murder anybody
today
I did not murder anybody
in the past
I will not murder anybody
in the future
most likely

in saying that
I have thought about it
many times
in relation
to many people

just as many people, I am sure
have thought
about murdering me

yet here I sit
typing this poem
and they are out there
somewhere
walking around
with their mouths open
or sitting at a table
chewing loudly

what a fucking nightmare

Rising, Rising

There is silence
something that I do not mind
usually

but today
I have no use for silence
and so, music

loud, louder, until
there is only music

a flood of music
soaking the carpet
slipping under the dishwasher
into the cracks in the tiles
lapping at the underside
of the windowsills
rising, rising
up my trouser legs
cloaking, pressing itself
urgently against me

louder still, until
it is horchata
sweet and smooth on my tongue

until it is wet blue smoke
that I inhale
empty, full, drowning

afterwards, barefoot
I step outside
into the winter
just to feel the cold

12th October 2021 –
The Last Throes of Summer

I hang the clothes
the cats purring at my feet
the washing line squeaking
the day waiting

I walk to the sally tree
bend my head
under branches that hang
almost to my waist
there is no wind
but the branches creak
all the same

I look up
to my daughter's treehouse
unused, almost, this summer
I see her rope ladder
the cot bolted to a bough
a heart carved in the bark
wept sap shining

I lean back a little
look straight up
at the cathedral of branches
splitting the sun
I close my eyes
knowing

that the light falls
in ribbons and shards
on my face and on my shoulders
and on the grass
all around me

Pulsing, Pulsing, Slowly

The hillside is mine
is soft beneath me
there is a weight
to the silence
that I breathe into

the day has gone
evening has come
falling quick-slow
and I
am still here

I am alone, but
there are others
hurrying from here
to there
in the city below

it suits me
being apart from it all
it suits them
being apart from me
this is what I tell myself

there is a distant light
beyond it all
pulsing
pulsing
slowly

hypnotically
mirroring my heartbeat
it might be a lighthouse
but it is hard to tell
from where I am

Winding, Empty

Late, warm, quiet
we sit on the balcony
reading, sipping, talking

beneath us
Spanish streets
winding, empty

above us
the moon a wrecking ball
demolishing the dark

The Stranger

The shock of seeing a stranger
inside your home
the expected
destroyed utterly
by the unexpected

a person
you have never seen before
walking down the hall
climbing up the stairs
standing in the kitchen

a person
generating fear
simply by inhabiting
a space
not meant for them

panic first, and then
a decision
the decision
fight
or flight

both options
long beyond my father
whom the stranger
visits
daily

The Pull
of the Earth

The grass is soft
I lie flat on it
feeling the pull
of the earth

the sky is grey
lit to white
intermittently
by bolts of lightning

rain falls steadily
cold steely drops
unrelenting
cleansing

no, I lie

the grass is carpet
heavy with water

the sky is the ceiling
dripping, dipping, bulging

the lightning is cracks
stretching, connecting

the rain is water
from the bath, overflowing

no, I lie
on the carpet
waiting for the sky to fall

Hustling, Bustling

Dublin was dark and wet
the rain rolling down
the back of my neck, and me
letting it

people hustled and bustled
hurrying
to wherever it was
they were hurrying to

I had nothing to do
nowhere to be
so, when I came upon the fire breather
I stopped

he was stripped to the waist
heavily tattooed
with ornate rings
on every finger

I do not remember his act
only the fire
wild and out of place
pluming upwards

people passed by
hustling, bustling
yet there was a time
they would have marvelled

a time he would have entertained kings
as a sorcerer, a necromancer
a tamer
of the untameable

I left him there, after a while
but I saw him, his fire pluming
over my shoulder, as I walked
through Temple Bar

as I walked through Merchant's Arch
as I walked along the quays, and
after all these years
I can still see him

Are You There?

She wears autumn colours
usually
but today she wears blue
light blue

she is aware, even as it passes
that her workday will fall
into that great vat of other workdays
to be stirred and stirred and rendered
into one

the traffic is bad
the bus is full but there is room enough
for her to stand
a man steps back on to her foot
he apologises profusely
she likes his smile

instead of the lift
she walks the four flights of stairs
to her apartment
she likes to keep in shape

her cat wakes, briefly, as she enters
the air is still and stale
she opens the window above the sink
a large bird flies across the sky
she watches it until it is lost to her

she heats up some lasagne
to push around her plate
she runs a bath as evening falls
undresses and enjoys the air against her
she tests the water
it has not heated, it is cold

she sits on the couch in her dressing gown
her legs beneath her
she skips from channel to channel
unsure of what she is looking for
the phone rings and she pads across the room
looking at the clock: 11.20 p.m.
she takes the phone from the receiver
places it against her ear
a voice at the end of the line says
'Sorry I'm calling so late. One of those days. Happy birthday.'
silence
'Can you hear me? Are you there?'

Nights Like These

There is a time of the night
when time becomes fluid
starts to fray
ripples and sways
when a part of you believes
that the night will last for ever

when the edge of the world is a haze
and blurring letters, emancipated insects
scuttle on pages

when it is impossible to tear your gaze away
from infomercials
and eighties hits
and B and C and D movies
yet

I find myself contented in this half doze
and I am sure that I will sleep well
if I can find it in me to drag myself
off the couch away
from this carnival of drivel

I promise I will shuffle down to bed
as soon as I watch the man
chop the mid-air pineapple in half
one more time
although

wait
look at how long that hose is extending
one minute it is neatly coiled
the next
the man in the purple polo shirt is hosing begonias
in Tim
buk
fucking
tu

I stand up and begin
the a.m. shuffle
towards tomorrow
life is here
life is there
waiting for me
and this is what I do with it

Standing in Mid-Air

For Paul Buchanan

His voice is ice
cracking

a wind
resting

a hailstorm
ending

his voice is porcelain
breathing

a leaf
falling

embers
fading

his voice is the land
sighing

broken glass
crunching

a mirror
misting

his words
are everything
else

The Party

I stand in the corner
drink in hand
a prop, really
something to swirl
something to look at
I look up, for a cursed half second
and catch eyes with someone

they smile
knowingly
I return that knowing smile
while wondering how heavy
a small handgun would feel in my hand
while dreaming of shooting each one
of their gleaming, white teeth
right out of their head

then that familiar bolt of reality strikes
I remember that I do not own a gun
have never even held one
that I, that no one, would be an accurate enough shot
that inevitably, the new carpet
would be ruined

The Shape of the Sea

It was not the moon that I stared at
but its reflection
showing me the faraway shape of the sea

I stood on the promenade, alone
feeling the gentle press
of a sultry Portuguese breeze

I wondered how the cats were
if they missed us
if they knew
were sure
that we would return to them

my wife and daughter came
to stand either side of me
my daughter held some candyfloss
'They don't call it candyfloss here, Dad.'
'Is that right? What do they call it?'
'I don't know.'

I smiled over her head at my wife
my wife smiled back
I picked up my daughter and placed her on the promenade wall
she leaned her back against me
I took a breath

the air was candyfloss sweet
the moon hung in the sky

the ocean stretched out before us
and somewhere beyond it
the cats were sleeping
were waiting

The Heron

I look out of the car window
across night fields

squinting, I can see
all my unlived lives

I drive on, into the village
into the rain

a traffic light turns red
I see Picasso people
walking in the raindrops
running down the window

the crescent moon is thin
a fingernail clipping
pointless, almost
there are no stars

a canal-bank heron becomes illuminated
by the headlights
as I pass

I wonder why
it is not afraid

Twine and Brown Paper

He handed it to me
a small parcel
wrapped with twine and brown paper
it wasn't Christmas
or my birthday
but I took it all the same

I untied the knot
peeled back the paper
to find a simple box
of polished walnut
I looked at him
he smiled with anticipation and
with his eyes asked me to open it

I lifted the lid
to find nothing
nothing at all
I looked at him
he, still smiling
told me to look again

at the bottom of the box
what I had thought to be a shadow
was something else
dark, pitch dark
the purest absence of colour
I have ever seen

I reached in
took it between my fingers
a two-by-two-inch swatch
of deep, deep black
faintly warm, strangely weightless

he looked left and right, leaned in
whispered that it was a piece
of the night sky
I asked him what I should do with it
he smiled and shrugged
whatever I liked
so I ate it

I thought that it might taste of liquorice
or the darkest of chocolate
but really
it tasted of nothing
nothing at all

A Poem from My Father
to My Daughter

I am an old man
you are still a little girl
hair the colour of cinder toffee
eyes the colour of nothing else
you look at me
ask a question
sure, absolutely sure
that I will have the answer
when I do not
you are disappointed
do not understand
and I tell you
that is OK
because neither do I

Snowflakes in the Long Grass, the Last Letter from Sylvia Welter to J.D. Salinger

I watched you through the gap in the curtains
standing beside the car
holding a letter
you looked unsure
it scared me
you stood so still
tall and greying, still

the sky was white
you shook your head against it
ripped the letter in half
in half again
and again
and again

when you flung it upward I lost it for a moment
white on white
I felt cold
watched the pieces fall as snowflakes
landing in our long grass
you were quiet when you came inside
even when I smiled my best smile

later, I snuck outside in my nightdress
my bare feet wet from the dew-damp grass
a charge in the evening air

I looked for snowflakes
as my eyes adjusted, they appeared to me
all through our long grass
I picked up three softening pieces
put them up my sleeve before
a gunshot, your voice ringing from the doorway
rolling down and through the Cornish hills

the handwriting was spindly
broken spider's legs said
'...ly when I was with yo...'
'...think of me?'
'Sylvia Welter.'
I dared to ask
you looked at me, furious
amazed
told me that you hadn't opened the letter
told me that she was nobody
the next morning, I looked through the gap in the curtains
all of the snowflakes were gone

The Day the Music Died

She sings in her room
at the top of her lungs
the sound
a joyous vapour
slipping under the door
through the keyhole
down the hall
to find me
in the kitchen

'American Pie'
a song written forty years
before she was born
about the deaths of Buddy Holly
Richie Valens and The Big Bopper
their plane crashing
on February 3rd, 1959

'the day
the music
died'

she sings in her room
at the top of her lungs
proving the song
a lie

Stirring the Milk into Her Tea

It still does not seem real
his death
she still stirs the milk into her tea
sipping it on the couch
each evening

she still hums quietly
while brushing her teeth
still edges the lawn
waves to the neighbours
cheerfully answers the phone

it swells in her sometimes
an enormous tide
that she swallows back down
reminding herself
that he would not want

for her to be engulfed
taken under
washed away
that he would want her
to be OK, to continue

she remembers his last gallery show
how people toasted him
looked at him with something
like awe
as she did

the paintings lie stacked now
dozens of them
the shed is damp, and she is worried
that they may be lost
beyond saving

she makes weekend plans
to walk to the back of the garden
to open the shed door
to see what might be saved
the weekends come and go

Superpowers

'What superpower would you choose?'
my daughter asked
as birds chirped
in the evening garden

I knew that her question
was not a question
but more an invitation
to ask her the same

so I did
'Invisibility!'
'And flight!'
I raised my eyebrows, waited

'That's two… OK… flight!
What about you?'
I had planned to choose flight
as these days I am more aware than ever

of gra
        vity

'I would like the power to assign sounds.'
she raised her eyebrows, waited
I explained
that I would like to designate sounds

that raindrops would become piano notes
and rainstorms haphazard symphonies
trees would sway as violins
that thunder would be purring

that car alarms would all be poems
whispered
by Morgan Freeman

that breaking glass would be
a baby's giddy squeal

that balloons would burst
not with a bang
but with a moo

'What sound would you give love?'
I thought about it
'A car crash.'
she punched my arm

The Crow

It hit the grille of the car
I did not feel it, barely heard it
but it was big, meaty
for a crow

it flew as though catapulted
from the roadside ditch
a ribbon of night sky
on a breezy sunny day

inert in the rear-view mirror
one wing, obviously broken
pointed up, straight up
at what had been left behind
what had been stolen

I drove on, tried to put it aside
tried not to think
about hatchlings waiting
starving

hours later, on the way home
I looked across
a thousand tyres
had rendered it an oily black paste

four or five crows stood around it
as if in discussion
picking at what was left

as I drove past
they flew away

Innocents

Imagine
if he had to face them
all at once
God, I mean
imagine them
resurrected
as he once was
those he had wronged
for no reason at all
other than the fact
that he works
in mysterious ways

imagine the impossible anger
of the innocents
who never had a prayer
those born into slavery
AIDS babies
cancer kids
the little girl raped for days and months
and years and years and years
by her swim instructor
her teacher
her uncle
her father
the little boys
forced to bow and kneel
in sacristies
shaded cloisters

to be touched
in holy places

imagine the incandescent fury
of those born blind, deaf, mute
born paralysed
limbless
broken
to broken-hearted parents
born dying
born dead
the tortured, downtrodden
the oppressed
those discriminated against
for no damn reason at all
the old lady
terrorised
for kicks
the old man
snapped in two
for the roll of cash in his sock drawer
the children born, bred
to be used
to be *used*
by men
by women
who were children once, too

imagine
the whole world shaking
as they come
for him
hundreds of millions

of hundreds of millions
and even God
all powerful
as he is
will surely go down
will surely drown
in the infinite body
the never-ending mass
of rage and frenzied sadness

it won't happen, of course
the game is rigged
has been from the start
either way
get down on your hands and knees
put your ear to the ground
hold your breath
still your heart
and listen
as well as you can
to the laughter

Judging a
Poetry Competition

His tone is curt, bruised
I let him talk
wait for him to get to the point
it doesn't take long

having read one of my books
he had called me out of the blue
a couple of months before
asking me to judge a poetry competition
flattered as I was
I had agreed

now, he mentions a poem
I acknowledge it
'I see that you didn't shortlist it.'
'OK.'
'Why not?'

there had been hundreds of poems
good and bad
I could remember some of them but
not that one
I go through the files
find it
barely remember it second time around

'I have the poem here.'
'Right, right, right.'
'It is coherent, but it says nothing.'
'Right, right, right.'
'I don't know why the writer felt the need to write it.'
'Right, right, right.'
'Everybody knows that flowers are nice.'
'That meadows are nice.'
'Right, right, right.'
'When I finished reading it, I did not feel anything.'
a pause
'The thing is, and maybe you didn't know this
but she works for RTÉ, and
is married to a famous journalist.'

I did not know, let it hang there for a while
'...OK.'
'Did you not feel that it had any merit at all?'
he goes on, before asking for my academic credentials
my literary qualifications
the conversation ends shortly after
when I tell him I have none

Barely December

You are missing a strip of hair
above your right ear
it draws me to your earlobe
hanging low
losing
to time and gravity
we sit in the sitting room
you, wearing your winter jacket
cold
shrunken
dishevelled
on the couch

you are reading something
your lips moving in silence
then stopping
you close the book
tightly
you try to speak but
your voice drowns
in a dam burst of memories
that come to rest just behind your eyes
you look at me
unable to breathe
your face an apology

I want to reach for you
but with your eyes
you ask for time

we wait
you manage to say
'It was Christmas…'
before your voice
turns to sand
and tears
heavy with salt
are brushed away
unwanted
on the back of your hand

you close your eyes
you clear your throat
yet still you cannot speak
I ask you what has happened to the hair
above your ear
you smile
glad to be rescued
'Your mother,
she forgot to adjust the hair clippers.'
we laugh
you point at the television
where a man demonstrates
an extendable hose
that he sprays in an arc
over a perfectly manicured garden
the grass is lush
'Why isn't my grass like that?'

we have dinner
my daughter gleefully pulls Christmas crackers
that you have bought for her
even though

it is barely December
you don't eat much
you still wear your winter jacket
you tell me that the cold
is inside you
the lines on your face
are many and deep
you are eighty-one years old
you are tired

we finish our dinner before the others
and return to the sitting room
the snooker is on
the crack of the balls
the whispered commentary
it could be thirty years ago
when you were a man
that didn't cry
and I was the boy
that you adopted, and loved
right away
I ask you
gently
what you had been thinking about earlier
you look puzzled
'It was Christmas…'
you try
I watch you try
'I can't remember.'

the crack of the balls
the whispered commentary
my daughter telling awful jokes badly

in the other room
I look over at you
smaller still and slumped
into your winter jacket
the collar raised high above your neck
the hairless strip above your right ear
the skin there perfect
pale and soft
you are asleep
it is barely December

Oranges, Reds
and Yellows

On the ground
swirling leaves reveal
the shape
of the wind

oil rainbows
in puddled water

streetlights flickering
waking early

collars up
heads down
against the wind

the electricity
the fizzing sulphur
of Halloween

black nights
black mornings
grey days

pressing myself
against the radiator

blowing warm air
into cupped hands

early talk of Christmas
pulsing ache for spring

Purgatory

The priest stood at the top of the classroom
his weekly visit
he talked to us about miracles and sin
we listened
at the end he asked if we had any questions
somebody asked about heaven, hell
and purgatory
this was a new one on me
purgatory
I put my elbows on my desk
leaned forward

the priest said that heaven was above us
hell below, with purgatory
the in-between
I felt my hand shoot up
he looked in my direction, nodded
I asked him what we do in purgatory
he said that we spend lifetimes there
thinking about our sins
he smiled as he said it
as if that was enough
I had more questions
but thought the better of them
having travelled those roads before
every one a cul-de-sac

for years I was afraid
knowing that each sin

each ungodly thought
was earning me more time
more lifetimes
in purgatory

today we spent some time in the garden
I cut trees for firewood
my wife trimmed the straggly branches
my daughter threw the straggly branches into the field
afterwards, we hung solar lights and wind chimes
a good spring day

now I sit at the kitchen table
a glass of fizzy black grape in my hand
an empty plate before me
the wind chimes sounding far away in the dusk
the solar lights catching my eye as they shimmer on
and I look out the window
at the in between

Feeding the Ducks in Naas, County Kildare

The sign said
DO NOT FEED BREAD TO THE DUCKS
apparently they cannot digest it properly
it makes them unwell
causes algae in the water
algae that brings disease
that harms the ducks
kills the fish

I thought back to my childhood
ducks and swans in a frenzy
the water almost boiling
flapping scrambles
for scattered bread
wet confetti

I felt a tug at my waist
looked down
three years old
wild sprung curls
her smile a universe
'Bread please!'

The sign said
PLEASE ONLY FEED THE DUCKS
HALF-CUT SEEDLESS GRAPES
CHOPPED LETTUCE
BIRDSEED

PEAS
CORN
OATS
I read it to her
watched her deflate

in the shop they had no grapes
no chopped lettuce, birdseed, corn or oats
only peas that she held as a prize
out in front of her
as we returned to the ducks
I helped her open the bag
watched her reach inside, take a handful
jump up and down as she threw them
they landed all around the ducks
ducks that didn't move
didn't bat an eyelid
or a wing
she tried again
some of the peas hit the ducks
landed on their backs
no movement, no interest

I felt a tug at my waist
looked down
'Bread please!'
I had picked up a few things in the shop
tomatoes, peppers, milk
bread
I reached into the plastic bag
opened up the bread
pushed past the heel
gave her one slice

in silence she tore it
into many careful pieces
flung them high into the air
watched them fall as
'Snow!'
before
flapping scrambles
ducks and swans in a frenzy
water boiling

Rocking Chair

I found you on your front lawn
you had asked me over
you never asked me over
but you had asked me over

you were sitting on a rocking chair
and though there didn't seem to be much to look at
you were looking
I sat beside you

'A rocking chair?'
        'A rocking chair.'
'Rocking chairs are for old people.'
        'I know.'
'You're not old.'
        'I know.'

Silence came and sat with us
we three
looking at nothing
but sky and distant headlights

'So why am I here?'
        'Why are any of us here?'
'Ha ha.'
        'Ha ha.'

you still hadn't looked at me

'I would have liked to grow old.'
        'Hey, it's happening, and there's not a whole lot
        we can do about it.'

you told me then

cancer

all through

not long

I cried
you didn't

we talked of greying
becoming distinguished
of bedside dentures and lollygagging
of waving our canes and shouting
'Get off my lawn!'

we talked of peeling humbugs and bullseyes
from sticky brown paper bags
how you never had the chance to smoke a pipe
we talked of little voices calling us
'Grandad.'

we talked
we talked and not once did you look at me
we aged together
got old
until the grass got damp

on the way home I stopped off
bought a pipe
some tobacco
for next time

I never went back

Never-Ending Tiny Mirrors

We are 2,000 miles from home, but
bad news is nothing
if not determined
we learn of illness, and
like a midday shadow
those miles lengthen

'Things are fine
things will be grand
stay where you are
we'll be in touch
he cannot talk
he is resting now
yes, he ate something today
try not to worry
things are fine...'

the afternoon slinks by
and in the pool we play
her snorts and shrieks contagious
the antidote to guilt

afterwards we walk, and I let her lead
her eager stride purposeful, determined
a secret path, two hopping frogs
and then
a sprawling bed of quartz laid out before us
sprinkled, with never-ending tiny mirrors
reflecting pieces of ourselves
we cannot hope to see

Feeding

She won't eat
I half fill the plastic spoon
with some sort of mush from a jar
it is orange
orange-ish
doesn't smell great
she won't eat
I don't blame her

I resort, finally, to swooping it
down to her
an airplane
coming in to land
on the runway of her tongue

her eyes follow it intently
I hear myself making engine noises
wondering if it will work
wondering if her lips will part
they do not
the airplane crashes softly
against her closed mouth
a tiny tragedy

I make the sound of an explosion
the sound of the passengers screaming
as they plummet
down her bib

I make smoke and fire with my fingers
rising up above her head

she looks at me
having no idea what an airplane is
I look at her
having no idea how to be a father

Howth Head,
Nearly Forty Years Ago

We walked up Howth Head
nothing to you then
you smoked a cigarette
the bliss on your face
as you sucked it in
and down
while telling me
to never start

I'm sure that we talked
sitting at the top
looking out over the sea
but what we said
is lost to me
and to you
now

I hadn't wanted to come
but you cajoled me into it
I remember being glad
I remember the sea, the scale of it
I remember being afraid
of the sheer enormity

your trousers were a dull blue
your hair was still black, mostly
your hands were big

big and rough
from the wood and the work
they were strong
they made me feel strong

after a while you stood up
said that we should get back
before the sun set
before the grass dampened
I remember that I didn't want to leave

Her Face to
the Sun

Summer has come
warm winds move around us, against us
we sit in the garden

she has a little ketchup
at the side of her mouth
a hotdog remnant

she closes her eyes
tilts her face to the sun
becomes a holy thing

I ask her how school was
she tells me that it was fine

I ask her if she enjoyed the barbecue
she tells me that she did

I ask if she would like to watch a film later
she says that she doesn't mind

I point at the bird feeder
at the line of birds perched on the branch
waiting for their turn
in pecking order, literally
she turns to see
turns back

smiles and nods and says
that they are beautiful

there is a distance between us
that was not there before
it is destroying me

Fabric

The best day of your life might not be a lottery win
it might not be when you got that girl
or that guy
it may not be your wedding day
the birth of your child
it might be a day when the early morning cloud
burns off, over a few sizzling lunchtime minutes
when you are a boy again
perched in a tree
sawing through a bough
that splits the air as it falls
allowing the tyre swing to carry
her twirling laughter
unencumbered
in all directions

it might be a day when a splinter goes in painlessly
and comes out easily
when the phone doesn't ring
not even once
when the bog is soft under our feet
and under the wheels of our bicycle tyres
another planet
inhabited by just us three
when the sunset is the wild brush strokes
of a drunken painter
when the wood burns in spits and sparks
the heat on our faces

the smoke knitting itself into the fabric of our clothes
when she announces, in her little voice
that she has finished her book
under the high stars in the low night
with the sun in the skies as the moon

Miniature
Mugs

I have two miniature mugs
gifts from my wife

one is red, and displays
The Flash emblem

the other is black, and displays
The Batman emblem

they are the perfect size
for double espressos

recently, I have learned
that filling them with boiling water

before making my coffee
ensures that the coffee

is hotter
for longer

while I wait for the kettle to boil
I unload the bottom shelf

of the dishwasher, and
while I wait for the mug to heat

I unload the top shelf
of the dishwasher

just now, somebody, somewhere
has fallen in love

Copper Water

The queue was not long
but it was slow
the elderly lady being served
determined to pay
with never-ending coins
that poured
as copper water
from her purse
to pool
on the countertop

the guy in front of me turned
smiled
threw his eyes up to heaven

I smiled back
trapped as I was

he started talking then
though about what
I cannot recall

nor can I recall
what he wore
the colour of his eyes
the timbre of his voice

in a court of law
I would commit to saying

that he had brown hair
did not wear glasses
and nothing more

just one of those guys
bland, inane, forgettable

I have no doubt
that he thought the same
about me

There, There

I tried to say the right thing
find the right words
to comfort, to reassure

instead, I offered platitudes
a there, there
a hand on your shoulder

the end had been sudden and
for you
unexpected

you recalled the conversation
asked me if I thought
there was a way back

she had called you to the kitchen
where she held a tea towel
and a cup

it was different, she was different
and you knew
even before she opened her mouth

'We have nothing.'
'We have each other…'
'What's the difference?'

you looked down at your fingernails
repeated it once
twice, three times

asked me again
if I thought
there was a way back

I tried to say the right thing and
more than that
tried to feel the right thing but

all that I could think
as you sat there, hunched and broken
was, that's a hell of a line

Just Before Midnight, Summer

She came running to me
a revelation
hiding
just behind her smile

she told me that the whole night
is just a shadow

I nodded

which means that daytime shadows
are just pieces of night

I agreed

her smile faltered
she said that it is a shame
the reverse does not happen

that she would love
if pieces of day
appeared in the night

I held out my arms
she jumped into them
her hair smelled like sunshine

The Same

It was the same drive
in the same car
on the same road

but

it was not the same

the verges, the trees
the signposts, the canal
all different
in ways
that went beyond
my ability to understand

that I was unable
to process then

that I am unable
to explain now

I returned home
opened the front door
to hear a call
'Is that you?'
I wasn't sure

4.35 a.m.

I sit on the toilet
woken, halfway through the night
by my stomach

my cotton-wool brain yields no answers
a regular breakfast, a regular dinner
no reason at all
for this

I run the day over
as best I can
the school run
the housework
the shopping
a phone call made
one received

I think of my interactions
my wife, my daughter

a wave to someone
while driving

'hello, thank you, goodbye'
while paying for the groceries

my father, by phone, twice

it is 4.35 a.m.
he is asleep now
they all are

All of the Night and
Most of the Day

He does not eat
any more
taking only a cup of tea
now and again
to appease my mother

he sleeps all of the night
and most of the day

much has been taken, stolen
from him, and
he knows
that while *he* sleeps
Dementia
does not

that while his appetite
evaporates
Dementia
will be ravenous
always

and so he fights
grits his teeth and fights
with the only weapon he has left
knowing that this time
to be beaten
is to win

An Afternoon with
My Father

We sit together
passing a sunny afternoon
the silences are long and easy
the best kind

I ask him questions, now and then
he answers them, now and then
though, often, it feels
as if I am pulling him back
from somewhere

somewhere better
than here
maybe

after a few hours
I stand to leave
he looks at me suddenly
tells me
that he remembers
that he remembers me
I am glad
I remember him too

1851

Her hip presses against the railing
Ireland still before her
close enough to touch
almost

she tries not to blink
against the sea air
tries to burn the distant Dublin Mountains
as a photographic negative
just behind her eyes

the ticket had been expensive
had cost most of what she had
but the blight had come
years before, and showed
no signs of leaving
leaving her
with only one decision

she knows it will be hard
that the streets will not
be paved with anything
other than flagstones

she turns slightly
her belly brushing the railing
flat, for now
she listens
for the secret heartbeat

thinks that she can hear it
echoing her own

the foghorn sounds
she straightens, startled stiff
the ship begins to move
very slowly
from the port wall
Ireland starts to become smaller
she looks away

Plastic Flowers

Killing time in a shop
I move slowly
from shelf to shelf
for almost an hour
deciding on which
of the plastic flowers
is most realistic

a strip-light flickers
in the far corner behind me
I find myself trying
to predict the flickering
as if there is a rhythm
some sort of pulse
there is not

I leave, walk into the car park
it is damp and pitch dark at 6.30 p.m.
an old lady struggles
to detach one trolley from the others
I walk over to help
she sees me and becomes afraid
I realise that the car park
is deserted and I understand

I try to reassure her with a smile
quickly free the chain and step back
she takes the trolley
thanks me, and hurries away

I start to walk towards my car
the air is thick, and my legs are heavy
I look up at the sky, sure
that it is falling
that this is the time of last things

all around me there are ghosts
their mouths open and they close
but I hear nothing

Loud

You could say that we were moving
three lanes of us curving slowly
towards the end of the world

it was hot outside
as hot inside
even with the windows open

the guy in the car next to mine
had his windows open too, and
his music on

loud

we inched forward while I
thought about different types
of murder

people walked by
walking their dogs
one man stopped

his dog raised his haunches
slightly
I knew what that meant

the man pulled a small plastic bag
from his pocket
he waited, we waited

the dog trembled slightly
it was an old dog, and, for a while
nothing happened

I wondered about colour, texture, size
as he waited, we waited
as the old dog trembled

then, it was over
diarrhoea, and
plenty of it

the man gave the dog a rub
put the plastic bag back into his pocket
and walked into the sun

On the Quays,
a Year Ago

It is a small car park
set on a wedge of scrap-land
between two buildings
on the quays

he was a small man
with a hi-vis vest
over his jacket

the meter was faulty
would not accept my fiver
he came over
said that it was
temperamental

his accent was hard
to pin down
Eastern European, maybe
so I asked him
where he was from

he hit the meter
hard
with the palm of his hand
once
twice
three times

then looked at me
answered, with a smile
'Far away,' and
was gone

he is probably there
right now
under the high sun
in Dublin City

21st December 2019

Four people have told me
so far
that today is the shortest day of the year
it was declared, each time, with an odd solemnness
followed, with reserved optimism, by a variation of
'Tomorrow the days will start to get longer.'
four people
I listen
nod
agree
without the heart to tell them
that tomorrow
will be just as short as today

Flags

Flags should be outlawed
take them down
burn them up
the flag
is *us*
and you can't have *us*
without *them*
and
let's face it
nothing good
ever came
from *them*
and
/
or
us

Fly Me to the Moon

You would complain about your hip
grimace as you caught a frisbee on the half-turn
there was breathlessness too
and you
would hum and scat your way up the stairs
to mask it
unwittingly creating
the soundtrack to my childhood

I remember your first grey hair
how we laughed
how you chased us
I don't remember your last black one

you told me once
how you think that you will never get old
until
one day
you do
I nodded, not really understanding
you ruffled my hair
not really understanding either

yesterday I tried to show my daughter a trick with a football
my knee, hit with an invisible crowbar, buckled
we lay on the grass
making daisy chains
while the pain went from boiling to a simmer

on Sunday mornings you would listen to 'Frank'
smile when I called it 'old fashioned music'
last week I heard 'Fly Me to the Moon'
for the first time
through your ears
and sensed our frames of reference
overlapping
as Time claws at us both

tonight, as I tucked her into bed
I told my daughter
how you think that you will never get old
until
one day
you do
she nodded
not really understanding
I brushed her cheek with the back of my hand
not really understanding either

I'm Just
the Ideas Guy

I've been lucky with the writing
poems published here and there
books on the shelves
which has led to people
telling me
what would make a good poem

a baby crying in the supermarket
'that would make a good poem'

an intricate design in cappuccino froth
'there's a poem in that for you'

a near miss while driving
'there's your next poem'

'you should write about happy things'
'you should write about dark things'
'you should write about what is happening in the world'
'you should write about your sister'

I tell people that I don't
that I can't
write to order
that I only write
what I want to write

I tell people that they should write
what *they* want to write
what *they* want to read
they shake their heads, baulk
explain to me that they have done the hard part
given me the ideas
it is then up to me to take them
run with them
craft them into poems
'and don't forget to give me credit!'

so, just to say
to everyone
that has done the hard work and given me
such incredible ideas
thanks
thanks a lot
I hope you like this poem

Nail Varnish

I sit on a wicker chair
my legs straight out
resting on the patio wall
my daughter studies my feet
mentions that the skin is soft
for a footballer
I give her a smile and think
that I haven't been a footballer
for a long time
and maybe never was

her eyes, wet fireworks
add to the light
of a sun
that shines through her curls
framing her face in a blaze
she has washed my feet
rubbed in lotions
now, she is going to paint my toenails

she lines them up
five small bottles
each a different colour
colours rich and deep despite the sunlight
she unscrews the first
the smell of it arrives
almost violently toxic
but intoxicating

I expect it to be room temperature
maybe even warm
but as she brushes it on
it is cold
my daughter talks to me
asks me how I am
how my day is going
if I have any holidays planned
mimicking the beauticians
from the television
the difference being
that with my daughter
the small talk
is enormous

Ding!

It wasn't there yesterday
I am sure of it
it arrived today
announcing itself
after I did a 'Find'
in Excel
that came up empty
Ding!
plaintive
chirpy
unwanted
I let it go
started a poem
finished a poem
saved it
Ding!
plaintive
chirpy
unwanted

I went online
people had the same problem
offered solutions
I tried them all
and still
Ding!
Ding!
Ding!

I wished for another sound
any other sound
nails down a blackboard
a scream
glass breaking
but no
Ding!
       Ding!
              Ding!
Ding! Ding! Ding! Ding!
Ding! Ding! Ding! Ding!
Ding! Ding! Ding! Ding!
Ding! Ding! Ding! Ding!

I tasted it in the back of my throat
swallowed it back down
murder
I don't know why
I am this way

The Flames

I don't know why I did it
an impulse, I suppose
I didn't even have much part in it
I just watched my hand
move away from me
towards the hearth

between my thumb and forefinger
was a fiver
crisp and new
ready to be spent
on groceries or clothes
or a set of sewer rods
to unblock the septic tank

I let it go
watched it fall
to rest on the turf
the fire waited for a half second
before taking it
hungrily
and then it was gone
I waited to feel something
a catharsis of some sort
anger at myself
at the waste
anything
but
I didn't feel a thing

a twenty had the same result
even the three fifties that I found
in the tin on the bookshelf
I gave them to the fire
and the fire took them
and my books
and my records
and all the food and the photographs in photo frames
and the chest of drawers and the television set
and the old toys and the fridge and the wardrobes
and the carpets and the floorboards and the bricks
and the rooftiles and the chimney and the mantel
and the clothes off my back
and the fire rose up
to lick the underbelly of the sky

I stood, close as I could stand
watched it slowly snarl back into itself
losing heat and light and anger
watched it until it was embers
smouldering
threatening to come alive again
with the touch of easy breezes
watched it until it was ash
quietly crumbling
losing shape and hope
watched it until it was nothing
lifeless
light grey and white
wisps of it curling away in the wind
I reached out
put my hand over it
it was still warm

A Poem from My Mother
to My Father

The way you stand
crooked, stooped
in doorways
unsure of where, why, what

the way you asked me
just last week
if we knew each other

the way I have to dress you
wash you
tell you
the time, the day, the season

the way you look at me
last thing
every night
is not
the way you looked at me
before

now, I tuck you in
seeing you
as your mother did
a boy again

now, I listen
to your apologies
quiet and stilted
yes, you are different now
no, you are not the man you were
before

I reassure you
remind you that I
am not the woman
that I was
either

the look you give me when I do
it is you
and I am me
and we are us
again

My Father Is Dead

Autumn walking and the world is red and yellow and fire orange and I am walking because there is nothing else that I can do or want to do and people do not notice me because I am trying my very best to be invisible and it is working and there is a weeklong dead badger on the side of the road and a waltzing balloon tied to the gate of a house and I am hungry but I do not want to eat and you are really gone and I miss you and the clouds are ghosts and you are everywhere

Unsaid

According to the literati
it is not what is said
but what is unsaid
that is important

that the art
of reading
is to read
between the lines

it all sounds
a little pretentious, but
worth a try
I suppose, so

Eimear
I

you

Acknowledgements

'Flickering' first published in *Tiny Wren Lit* in 2024

'The Pebble' first published in *Ink In Thirds* in 2024

'Bright Blue' first published in *takahē Magazine* in 2023

'Fishing Line' first published in *Creative Ireland Anthology* in 2022

'The Chevrolet' first published in *The Pomegranate* in 2023

'Sharing a Sink with John. B. Keane in a Pub Toilet in the Mid-Nineties' first published in *Short Édition* in 2022

'Room to Room to Room to Room' first published in *The Cormorant* in 2023

'In the Cutlery Drawer' first published in *Better Than Starbucks* in 2018

'Mount Carmel Maternity Ward, January 2012' placed second place in the Cisco Writer's Club Contest in 2021

'2013, Before Dementia' first published in *Ink In Thirds* in 2023

'Lunchtime in Dublin City' first published in *Stand Magazine* in 2025

'How to Raise a Daughter' first published in *The Bad Day Book* in 2025

'The Tin' first published in *Iceberg Tales* in 2019

'Traffic' first published in *The Antigonish Review* in 2024

'The Whistling Man' first published in *Terror House Magazine* in 2018

'A Match in Mount Merrion, Dublin, Twenty-Seven Years Ago' first published in *Plorkology* in 2025

'A Poem From My Father to My Mother' first published in *The Irish Times*, Runner-up in Stephen DiBiase Poetry Competition and published in *Every Day is a Fresh Beginning: Meaningful Poems for Life* in 2020

'A Dark Spot, Glistening' first published in *Northern Gravy* in 2022

'Sitting on a Bench, Waiting' first published in *Kinship* anthology in 2023

'A Worm in 1981' first published in *Fevers of the Mind* in 2020

'His Name Escapes Me Right Now, but It Might Come Back to Me Later' first published in *Fevers of the Mind* in 2020

'Midnight at the Petrol Pump' first published in *Paddler Press* in 2022

'Naming Snowflakes' first published in *Better Than Starbucks* in 2020

'Procrastinator' first published in *Steam Ticket* in 2022

'The Great Writer and His Process' first published in *Steam Ticket* in 2022

'Fists' first published in *The Irish Times* in 2019

'Cables and Cement' first published in *Querencia Press* in 2024

'The Arcadia' first published in *Seaside Gothic* in 2024

'Watching an Independent Film With My Wife' first published in *The Pomegranate* in 2022

'When the Soil Is Flooded Worms Come to the Surface to Breathe' first published in *Firmament* in 2021

'That That' first published in *Bindweed Magazine* in 2023

'Sandalwood' first published in *Ethos Literary Journal* in 2018

'Sarah Goodwelles' first published in *City Brink Magazine* in 2020

'Dawn' first published in *Hibiscus Poetry Journal* in 2020

'School Visit, October 24th, 2019' first published in *New Croton Review* in 2025

'What Waits Around the Corner' first published in *Fowl Feathered Review* in 2024

'Diving' first published in *Poetry Ireland Review* in 2019

'Photograph' first published in *Westerly Magazine* in 2019

'My Birthday' first published in *Better Than The Times* in 2024

'Morocco' first published in *Door Is A Jar* in 2023

'Gentle' first published in *The Pomegranate* in 2023

'Hatch Street Years' first published in *Dreich Magazine* in 2020

'Herself' first published in *The Antigonish Review* in 2024

'Neon' first published in *The Alchemy Spoon* in 2023

'North Strand Summer – Seventy-Five Years Ago' first published in *Sans. Press* in 2024

'Boy A and Boy B' first published in *DarkWinter Literary Magazine* in 2022

'Seven Years Old' first published in *DarkWinter Literary Magazine* in 2022

'Breaths' first published in *The Phoenix* in 2019

'Winding, Empty' first published in *The Madrid Review* in 2024

'Nights Like These' first published in *Heliopause Magazine* in 2019

'Standing in Mid Air' recited on *The Last Word – Culture Club with Matt Cooper – Today FM* in 2024

'The Party' first published in *Heliopause Magazine* in 2019

'The Shape of the Sea' first published in *Last Stanza* in 2023

'The Heron' first published in *Short Édition* in 2022

'Twine and Brown Paper' first published in *Milk and Cake Press – Dead of Winter Anthology II* in 2022

'A Poem From My Father to My Daughter' first published in *Samfiftyfour* in 2025

'Snowflakes in the Long Grass, the Last Letter from Sylvia Welter to JD Salinger' placed third in the Anthony Cronin International Poetry Award in 2020

'Stirring the Milk ino Her Tea' first published in *The Pomegranate* in 2021

'Superpowers' first published in *Door Is A Jar* in 2022

'The Crow' first published in *Last Leaves* in 2023

'Innocents' first published in *The Soap Box Press* in 2022

'Judging a Poetry Competition' first published in *En Bloc* in 2022

'Barely December' first published in *Porridge Magazine* in 2019

'Oranges, Reds and Yellows' first published in *Saffron Coloured Rock Candy* in 2019

'Never Ending Tiny Mirrors' first published in *Evening Street Review* in 2019

'December 21st, 2019' first published in *Loft Books Anthology* in 2020

'Flags' first published in *Into The Void* in 2020

'Fly Me to the Moon' first published in *The Bollman Bridge Review* in 2020

'I'm Just the Ideas Guy' first published in *The Pomegranate* in 2022

'Nail Varnish' first published in *Dreich Magazine* in 2020

'Ding!' first published in *Firmament* in 2021

'The Flames' first published in *House of Zolo* in 2021

'A Poem From My Mother to My Father' first published in *Acumen* in 2025

'My Father is Dead' first published in *Acta Victoriana* in 2025

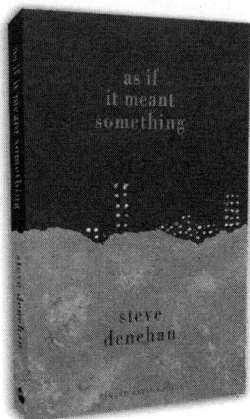